The Royal Mysteries

The Royal Mysteries

Rosary Meditations
from Jordan to Jerusalem

ROLAND WALLS

Illustrated by
Elizabeth Ruth Obbard

Darton, Longman and Todd
London

First published in 1990 by
Darton, Longman and Todd Ltd
89 Lillie Road, London SW6 1UD

Nihil Obstat Philip J. Kerr STL
Censor Deputatus
Imprimatur Keith Patrick O'Brien
Archbishop of St Andrews and Edinburgh
5 May 1990

The *Nihil Obstat* and *Imprimatur* are a declaration that a book or pamphlet is considered to be free from doctrinal or moral error. It is not implied that those who have granted the *Nihil Obstat* and *Imprimatur* agree with the content, opinions or statements expressed.

British Library Cataloguing in Publication Data

Walls, Roland
The royal mysteries.
1. Catholic. Christian life. Prayer. Rosary. Devotional works
I. Title
242.74

ISBN 0–232–51916–1

Phototypeset by Input Typesetting Ltd, London.
Printed and bound in Great Britain by
Courier International Ltd, Tiptree, Essex.

For Our Lady
of Mount Grace

Contents

Contents

Acknowledgements

This book is indebted to Fr Raymund Devas OP who, in his introduction to *Our Lady's Psalter* (CTS 1980), gives an account of the ways the Rosary has been said over the centuries. He re-introduces the old custom of reading a verse of scripture before each 'Hail Mary'. This method helps to make clear the words of Pope Paul VI in his exhortation, *Marialis Cultus* (1974): 'The Rosary is a Gospel prayer, centred on the mystery of the incarnation'.

The scriptural quotations are based on the New Jerusalem Bible, published and copyright 1985 by Darton, Longman and Todd Ltd and Doubleday & Co. Inc., and used by permission of the publishers.

Introduction

> Popular devotions of the Christian people should be so drawn up that they harmonise with the liturgical seasons, accord with the sacred liturgy and in some way derive from it and lead the people to it. (Vatican II constitution on the Sacred Liturgy 13)

I have waited twenty years before daring to suggest that five more mysteries could be added to the traditional fifteen. There is something outrageous in the very idea. It is like adding extra details to an old master, or extra notes to a Beethoven symphony. For the Rosary is a work of art. It already has a classic perfection of symmetry and proportion. How does one excuse such temerity? My excuse is twofold.

First. Almost at my first introduction to the Rosary, as a schoolboy nearly sixty years ago, I was conscious of the gap between the last joyful mystery of Christ found in the temple at the age of twelve and the first sorrowful mystery of Christ at Gethsemane, and years later I asked myself whether there were any similar mysteries of Christ's ministry.

Secondly. This coincided with a movement of the Spirit in the church which gave rise to what is now known as 'Gospel Spirituality'. Whole communities have grown up with the desire to take the Gospels as their guide to faithful obedience. The new form of liturgy brings into prominence the significance of the Gospel and the homily as the climax of the ministry of the word.

There seems then to be a renewed reflection on the mystery of Christ on his way to the Father and on his way towards us as he goes to the Father. Is it possible that such reflection can be incorporated into the well proven use of the Rosary? Any suggested incorporation must take account of two fundamental features of the devotion.

The Rosary is a meditation prayed with and through the thoughts of Mary the Mother 'who kept all these things and pondered on them in her heart'. It is also an involvement in prayerful reflection on mysteries which have their liturgical celebrations in the church's calendar. Any supplement to the fifteen mysteries must conform to these two aspects of the devotion. Are there then five Gospel mysteries which correspond to and complete the joyful, sorrowful and glorious mysteries?

I believe there are five such which may not inappropriately be called the 'Royal Mysteries'. They stand out like icons – indeed they have often been the subject of icons (perhaps a third characteristic of the mysteries of the Rosary). I suggest they are the following:

1. The Baptism of Christ
2. The Temptation of Christ
3. The Transfiguration of Christ
4. The Entry of Christ into Jerusalem
5. The Institution of the Eucharist

They are all mysteries of Christ revealing to us who he is and therefore what he does. They are all high points in his ministry and would have been shared by the apostles with Our Lady before and after Pentecost, and they all are given high place in the liturgical celebrations of the church. They complete the series from the Annunciation of the Virgin Mary to the joy of Mary and all the saints in heaven. Above all, they conform to the characteristic of a mystery, that is they enfold us as we pray ourselves into them and they are mysteries of our redemption as persons in community, in communion with Christ and his Father, in communion with one another by the Holy Spirit, all made possible by that initial fiat of Mary to the proffered grace of God.

Each mystery is introduced by a short reflection, followed by ten scriptural verses which may accompany the ten 'Hail Mary's', and a short collect prayer concludes each decade which can be said before or after the 'Glory be to the Father'. The reflection, the scriptural verses and the collect are intended to help relate each mystery to the church's faith in Christ and its liturgical celebration.

For those who may be new to this way of praying, I have added two appendices which help to explain the mysteries more fully and give guidance on how to use the rosary.

1

The Baptism of Christ

We are so used to reflecting on the positive side of the baptism of Jesus – the voice of the Father and the overshadowing Spirit – that we are hardly conscious of the immense embarrassment this baptism of Christ by John caused the early Christian community. How did a sinless Christ line up with sinners to receive a baptism for the remission of sins? Only Matthew gives us an answer. John the Baptist is unwilling to baptise Jesus: in utter incredulity he asks, 'Do you come to me? I have need to be baptised by you'. Jesus answers, 'Let it be so now: so that everything that is God's will may be completed *or* so that we may achieve a complete vindication of God'. Jesus puts all the cards on the table. He has come to identify himself with sinners, to line up in the queue of those confessing their sins. He has come to separate himself from all religious self-righteousness and to take on himself the sins of the world. He declares by his baptism that he has come to be the Servant of the Lord of Isaiah 53 – the sinless lamb of God of John 1.36, where John the Baptist recognises and indicates 'the Lamb of God who takes away and bears the sin of the world'.

To do this sin-bearing – to join the company of sinners – is to fulfil God's will and vindicate the God of Israel who recognises his servant in whom he is well pleased and his beloved Son who brings the Father's love right down to those who most need it.

The voice of the Father and the descending Spirit constitute the witness of the one holy will of the Trinity to save sinners by sharing their lot, bearing their sins, and being identified with them in life and death. In life, by table fellowship with them to the point of scandal; in death, by being taken as a sinner and crucified as a common criminal between two thieves.

Now Christ is consecrated by the waters of Jordan and the Holy Spirit for the strange journey into a far country to share the lot of the Prodigal

Son and return with him to his Father's house – a journey that will cost him not less than everything. He is therefore acclaimed the true Son of the Father, a son whose consecrated humanity will be so utterly given for sinners that it will express as through clear glass the eternal glory of the self-giving Trinity. It will be completed by a baptism of blood.

There is only one baptism for the forgiveness of sins as the Creed confesses. The one baptism is the baptism of Christ in the Jordan which is now available to all who would follow Christ by the baptism of water and the Spirit. Consecrated by his consecration, accepted as sons with the Beloved, we sinners receive a new life of self-giving, of servants of the Lord who are removed from any self-righteous standing off from our fellow sinners. We share the identification of Christ with the fallen Adam in order to embrace 'on the level' our fellow sinners. So we take part in a huge operation of the self-giving, humble and humiliated God to win back those who have the long journey to make to their father's house. The one baptism says it all, contains it all, and consecrates us to a life of following the Lamb wherever he goes.

1 It was at this time that Jesus came from Nazareth in Galilee and was baptised in the Jordan by John (Mk 1.9).

2 John tried to dissuade him, with the words, 'It is I who need baptism from you, and yet you come to me!' (Mt 3.14).

3 And when Jesus had been baptised he at once came up from the water and suddenly the heavens opened and he saw the Spirit of God descending like a dove and coming down on him (Mt 3.16).

4 And suddenly there was a voice from heaven, 'This is my Son, the Beloved; my favour rests on him' (Mt 3.17).

5 I baptise you in water for repentance, but the one who comes after me is more powerful than I, and I am not fit to carry his sandals; he will baptise you with the Holy Spirit and fire (Mt 3.11).

6 Jesus replied: In all truth I tell you, no one can enter the kingdom of God without being born through water and the Spirit (Jn 3.5).

7 You cannot have forgotten that all of us, when we were baptised into Christ Jesus, were baptised into his death (Rm 6.3).

8 You shall know that I am Yahweh when I put my Spirit in you, and you revive (Ezk 37.14).

9 I shall pour clean water over you and you will be cleansed (Ezk 36.25).

10 I shall give you a new heart, and put a new Spirit in you; I shall remove the heart of stone from your bodies and give you a heart of flesh instead (Ezk 36.26).

Dear Father,
Your voice was heard at the Jordan
to awaken our faith in Jesus your Son;
the sinless numbered among the transgressors.
Your Spirit anointed him with joy,
to bring good news of salvation to the poor.
Give us who are baptised with his baptism,
his humility
and a share in his mission,
so that we may also share his joy,
for his holy name's sake. Amen

2

The Temptation of Christ

If the baptism of Jesus was the consecration to his work and mission, the temptation which follows immediately is the refusal to use any other means than his vulnerable, fragile humanity to achieve his task. Jesus refuses to use his privilege as Son of God to do anything that would compromise his complete trust in the Father. He refuses to witness to any other nourishment than the listening and feeding on the word of his Father. He will not provide bread for himself or anyone else in order to match up to the expectations of what the Messiah will do. Only out of compassion will he feed the crowd – but not out of self-pity will he feed himself. Even when he fed the crowd in the desert he immediately hid himself from those who would make him king. 'Test your designation of Son of God in order to get off the hook', says the devil. 'If he be the Son of God, let him come down from the cross and we will believe in him.'

The hungry are not fed in order that they may believe the Gospel, but the Gospel is preached so that the hungry may be fed – from compassion not by manipulation. Here, as in all three temptations, the verbal icon alludes to the three temptations of Israel in the desert. 'They demanded food in the desert', and they got it in the form of manna – the bread from heaven.

They twisted the arm of God in complete distrust of his care. 'Bread – how can he give us that?' Christ stands where Israel falls. He ends this temptation as each of them with a word from Deuteronomy: 'Man does not live by bread alone, but by every word which comes forth from the mouth of God.' The devil combs through the whole Bible to find a word to back up his proposal. Jesus sticks to what has been called the book of the heart of God – the heart broken by the repeated rebellions of his people.

We too with Christ will have our desert temptations – as the Messianic people did. And one will certainly be that of distrusting God our Father to provide us at his own time with what we so desperately need. We too with the church will be called into a desert to fast with Christ so that we may know our true food is the word of the Father.

The second temptation is a subtle one. Jesus is now asked to show his complete trust in God by throwing himself down from the temple, relying on the promise that God will not let him hurt his foot against a stone. But to do this is to tempt God, to try him out to see if he exists or is where we are. What looks like trust turns out to be mistrust – asking for a sign to be given so that we may know whether God is trustworthy.

This is a very common form of pious mistrust. As it was for Israel so it is for us a constantly recurring desire to make sure of God, by looking for, desiring 'a sign from heaven', which we imagine is a sign of our faith. Quite the contrary. Only 'an evil and adulterous generation looks for a sign'. Faith for Jesus, faith for us, has to be that curious ability to go on when God is not obvious, seemingly absent. Faith does not look for a sign from God or ask for one. Faith does not transfer its own testing on to God. 'You must not put God to the test.' That is the height of irreverence and the clearest indication of profound mistrust.

Jesus renounces all drama which would cow men and women into belief. He will win them by making the ordinary into the extraordinary, by his own trustful existence in a world where even the grass of the field is clothed by the Father, and even a sparrow does not fall to the ground without him knowing it.

The last temptation is a fierce one. 'Why not take the way of common sense. Born into a backyard of the Roman Empire, born in obscurity and local scandal, burdened by such a total mission, why not take the way of power like everyone else who has ever done anything worthwhile? Come on the side of influence, control, government, politics. Give your recognition to me. I have the battalions, the guns, the craftiness, to get you what you need – success. When you get into the saddle it's up to you what you do with your power – you could do so much good – and so quickly. You haven't a hope in hell if you go it alone. You will end up a pathetic clown if you go on with the quixotic idea that love conquers all. It obviously doesn't and won't. Save yourself the appalling end you will meet if you don't use common sense.'

This is the ever present temptation to Israel, to the church – to line up with centres of power and influence, to become one yourself. 'Join the world on its own terms in order to save it.'

Even Peter will bring this temptation again before Christ. 'Don't let yourself be crucified', and Jesus, remembering surely the third temptation, in anguish cries out, 'Get behind me, Satan, because you think as the world thinks'.

This is the final hurdle. In Gethsemane Christ in an agony conforms his human will to divine will in his repeated prayer. We too are at the end of a tragic misunderstanding following Constantine's offer of power, influence and rule to the Christians who inevitably misused it, and allowed a contradiction of Christ's message to be the means of proclaiming it. We are alive in a remarkable time when we are being asked corporately and individually to return to the Christ of the third temptation – to walk the way of self-giving nonentity so that the power of God can be set forth in weakness, in the folly of self-sacrificing love – the way of the Cross. This above all is what Satan cannot endure.

1 Then Jesus was led by the Spirit out into the desert (Mt 4.1)

2 He fasted for forty days and forty nights, after which he was hungry, and the tester came and said to him, 'If you are Son of God, tell these stones to turn into loaves' (Mt 4.2–3).

3 But he replied, 'Scripture says: Human beings live not on bread alone, but on every word that comes from the mouth of God' (Mt 4.4).

4 The devil then took him to the holy city and set him on the parapet of the Temple. 'If you are Son of God,' he said, 'throw yourself down; for scripture says: He has given his angels orders about you, and they will carry you in their arms in case you trip over a stone' (Mt 4.5–6).

5 Jesus said to him, 'Scripture also says: Do not put the Lord your God to the test' (Mt 4.7).

6 Next, taking him to a very high mountain, the devil showed him all the kingdoms of the world and their splendour. And he said to him, 'I will give you all these, if you fall at my feet and do me homage' (Mt 4.8–9).

7 Then Jesus replied, 'Away with you, Satan! For scripture says: The Lord your God is the one to whom you must do homage, him alone you must serve' (Mt 4.10).

8 For the high priest we have is not incapable of feeling our weaknesses with us, but has been put to the test in exactly the same way as ourselves, apart from sin (Heb 4.15).

9 Let us, then, have no fear in approaching the throne of grace to receive mercy and to find grace when we are in need of help (Heb 4.16).

10 For the suffering he himself passed through while being put to the test enables him to help others when they are being put to the test (Heb 2.18).

Dear Father,
Your Son was exposed to temptation,
as we are,
to leave the hard way of sacrifice
and renunciation of self.
Give us his strength to overcome
the enticements of the enemy,
and bring to perfection
the image of your Son within us
for the sake of his name. Amen

LISTEN TO HIM

3

The Transfiguration of Christ

So far the royal mysteries of the baptism and temptation have upturned all human ideas about royalty and kingship and radically altered what we usually think about authority and power. Christ's royal consecration and his kingly rule is about his royal loving solidarity with sinners, his rejection of external compulsion and manipulation, his choice of obedience and worship of the Father. Now, in what has been called the little climax of the Gospel, the momentary lifting of the veil, a foretaste of the Resurrection glory, the true meaning is given – the glory of such humiliation. In verses faith is given a glorious icon. Each detail is a stroke of the brush, a precious gem. The completed narrative of the transfiguration is a veritable *son et lumière* creation of great beauty. The inspiration of the Holy Spirit is seen most clearly in the production of this kind of narrative by the early Christians. Unique in literature, this writing is intended for contemplation, corporate and personal.

Here is the obverse of the precious coin of revelation. The true eternal value of the God who in Christ hides himself in identifying himself with us in all our fragility, insignificance even to death, is the God who by so doing transforms our nature with his own glory and majesty. By the way of solidarity and temptation he leads us into glory. He 'transfers us from the kingdom of darkness into the kingdom of his Son'.

1 Six days later, Jesus took with him Peter and James and John and led them up a high mountain on their own by themselves. There in their presence he was transfigured (Mk 9.2).

2 His clothes became brilliantly white, whiter than any earthly bleacher could make them (Mk 9.3).

3 Then Peter spoke to Jesus, 'Rabbi,' he said 'it is wonderful for us to be here' (Mk 9.5).

4 And a cloud came, covering them in shadow; and from the cloud there came a voice, 'This is my Son, the Beloved. Listen to him' (Mk 9.7).

5 Then suddenly, when they looked round, they saw no one with them any more but only Jesus (Mk 9.8).

6 And all of us, with our unveiled faces like mirrors reflecting the glory of the Lord, are being transformed into the image that we reflect in brighter and brighter glory; this is the working of the Lord who is the Spirit (2 Co 3.18).

7 It is God who said, 'Let light shine out of darkness' (2 Co 4.6).

8 It is God who has shone in our hearts to enlighten them with the knowledge of God's glory, the glory on the face of Christ (2 Co 4.6).

9 That is why we do not waver; indeed, though this outer human nature of ours may be falling into decay, at the same time our inner human nature is renewed day by day (2 Co 4.16).

10 Christ is the image of the unseen God (Col 1.15).

Dear Father,
You have revealed to us
the glory of your Son,
so that he may not miss
the glory of his Passion.
May we, and your whole church,
which is his body,
be faithful in suffering,
and be clothed at last
with the glory of the head
ever Jesus Christ our Lord. Amen

4

The Entry of Christ into Jerusalem

Each Palm Sunday the church encourages us to become little children, to act out a little child's play. We carry our palms, we take our part in a charade (child's play) of a royal procession. It is a poignant re-enactment of the original, absurdly inadequate demonstration for and acclamation of the King of kings on his royal way to his Passion and coronation with thorns. But that original little play-acting was actually the final straw which brought the religious and civil authorities to decide that Jesus must die. Unbelievably, they were threatened by this claim of the powerless king on the devotion of the crowd. It was the donkey that challenged them with being possibly inevitably unseated from their power and authority, and it is the same today.

What happens to church and society if royalty and power are really best shown in humanity and service, if God is really putting down the powerful from their thrones and exalting the humble? The authorities were sensible: the only thing they could do was to devise some means of getting rid of this man. It would happen again today. It does happen whenever the gentle Christ undermines the ecclesiastical and civil assumptions of the autocrats.

1 Then they took the colt to Jesus and threw their cloaks on its back, and he mounted it (Mk 11.7).

2 And those who went in front and those who followed were all shouting, 'Hosanna! Blessed is he who is coming in the name of the Lord!' (Mk 11.9).

3 He entered Jerusalem and went into the Temple (Mk 11.11).

4 He began driving out the men selling and buying there (Mk 11.15).

5 Does not Scripture say: My house will be called a house of prayer for all peoples? (Mk 11.17).

6 Jesus answered, 'Destroy this Temple, and in three days I will raise it up' (Jn 2.19).

7 But he was speaking of the Temple that was his body (Jn 2.21).

8 And suddenly the Lord whom you see will come to his Temple (Ml 3.1).

9 Who will be able to resist the day of his coming? Who will remain standing when he appears? (Ml 3.2).

10 Rejoice, exult with all your heart, daughter of Jerusalem. Yahweh is King among you, Israel, you have nothing more to fear (Zp 3.17).

Dear Father,
May we follow our humble King
into the heart of your church,
the holy city of Jerusalem
and sing in childlike simplicity
the praises of our King.
May Christ continually cleanse
the temple of the church
so that it may be a house of prayer
for all nations; for his name's sake. Amen

5

The Institution of the Eucharist

What Jesus did at the Last Supper is a miracle of compression. He adapted the familiar, universal elements of a meal – food and drink – and conveyed the whole of his message in an acted parable, universally understood but with a meaning beyond our comprehension. Bread and wine became transformed into a sign of his birth, life and death and resurrection. They became himself as he gives, shares, unites himself with and to us wholly and without remainder, to be eaten and digested and assimilated.

They became himself as he offers himself at the same time in life and death to his Father. By this simple act Jesus compressed into a moment all his meaning and as Julian of Norwich says 'Love was all his meaning'. Do this in remembrance of me – of me as I was born for you, as I grew up among you, as I ministered to you in healing, forgiving, teaching, as I suffered for you and as I died for you and rose again for you and invited you to follow me to glory. All is here, all we know of the Son, all we know of God the Father, all we know of where God the Holy Spirit is leading all and each of us on the way of the Cross to self-giving, self-renunciation, in a love which joins us to God and one another. 'In this unity is our salvation' (Julian of Norwich).

1 The disciples set out and went to the city and found everything as he had told them and prepared the Passover (Mk 14.16).

2 When evening came he arrived with the twelve (Mk 14.17).

3 And as they were eating he took bread, and when he had said the blessing he broke it (Mk 14.22).

4 He gave it to them. 'Take it', he said 'this is my body' (Mk 14.22).

5 Then he took a cup, and when he had given thanks he handed it to them, and all drank from it, and he said to them, 'This is my blood' (Mk 14.23–24).

6 The blood of the covenant, poured out for many (Mk 14.24).

7 It is my Father who gives you the bread from heaven (Jn 6.32).

8 The bread which comes down from heaven and gives life to the world (Jn 6.33).

9 I am the bread of life (Jn 6.48).

10 Whoever eats my flesh and drinks my blood lives in me and I live in that person (Jn 6.56).

Dear Father,
Your Son has given us a wonderful sacrament
as a memorial
of his Passion and death.
May we so venerate the sacred mysteries
of his body and blood,
that we may experience within ourselves
the fruit of his redemption
for his name's sake. Amen.

Appendix 1

The Mysteries

In present day English the word 'mystery' means an unsolved problem. Crime stories such as 'The Mystery of the Missing Bride' set out to solve the mystery. We say, 'It's a mystery how she manages to cope'. The mystery would disappear if we knew the secret. 'Mystery' in Holy Scripture and in the language of Christian tradition, however, means something that *has* been kept secret and now is revealed. Jesus spoke of the 'mysteries of the kingdom' (Mark 4.11) and St Paul uses the word to mean God's plan for our rescue from sin, meaninglessness and death (1 Corinthians 1.17, Colossians 1.26). He speaks of the 'mystery of Christ' now revealed to the apostles and prophets (Colossians 3.4) and proclaimed to everyone through the church. Christ is the central mystery and he gives a new and fuller meaning to actions and states of life, for example holy matrimony; in

Christ it becomes a 'great mystery' – the mystery, an open sign of Christ's union with his church (Ephesians 5.22). Mystery is therefore like a hitherto locked door to which we now have the key. We can now enter a new dimension of living and understanding. We are invited into a new space beyond our reason but accessible to faith. The mysteries enfold us, embrace us – we do not grasp them, they grasp us. From an early date the church called the sacraments mysteries because they are not only visible signs of the revelation but they encompass us – they give us the space and dimension of the kingdom.

By the phrase 'mysteries of the Rosary' we refer to the cardinal moments of the revelation which Christ achieved – the birth, infancy and childhood are the Joyful Mysteries; the sufferings and Passion are the Sorrowful Mysteries, the glory of the Resurrection, Ascension, Pentecost and the first fruits of the glory in Mary are the Glorious Mysteries.

This little book attempts to complete the series with five more – Royal Mysteries of the kingly ministry of Jesus during his active life. When we use the Rosary we enter each one of these doors into the kingdom life, we allow the mystery to interpret our lives, to solve our problems, to be the key that opens our minds and our hearts so that we begin to think as God thinks, to desire God's desires, to will God's will. We allow the Gospel to penetrate us, and to give rise to reflection and prayer controlled by the Gospel itself not just by our concerns and anxieties. It releases us from our prisons of self-preoccupation into the liberty and open air of the kingdom. Millions of Christians can testify to the ability of this form of prayer to raise them from tepid prayers of self-concern; it enables them to breathe again the fresh air of the Holy Spirit and pray the prayer of self-giving and self-surrender.

For those who use this book and are yet unfamiliar with the other mysteries, the following are the traditional fifteen mysteries (texts with each mystery to be found in *Our Lady's Psalter* by Raymund Devas OP, CTS 1980).

The Joyful Mysteries

1. The Annunciation to Mary
2. The Visit of Mary to Elizabeth
3. The Birth of Jesus Christ
4. The Presentation of Christ in the Temple
5. The Finding of the Boy Jesus in the Temple

The Sorrowful Mysteries

1. The Agony in Gethsemane
2. The Scourging at the Pillar
3. The Crowning with Thorns
4. The Carrying of the Cross
5. The Crucifixion

The Glorious Mysteries

1. The Resurrection
2. The Ascension
3. The Coming of the Spirit
4. The Homecoming of Mary (Assumption)
5. The Crowning of Mary and the Joy of the Saints

Appendix 2

The Rosary and how to use it

It seems that the Rosary as we know it developed out of a tender devotion to the humanity of Christ in the eleventh and twelfth centuries, with a corresponding devotion to his mother. This was taking place at the same time as the provision of a 'Psalter' for the laymen and women was taking shape. The one hundred and fifty Psalms of the choir office were replaced by one hundred and fifty Paters or 'Our Fathers' to constitute a Poor Man's Breviary, and strings of beads were provided to count them. A similar Psalter for Our Lady was introduced, consisting of one hundred and fifty 'Hail Mary's', with similar beads on which to count them. The 'Hail Mary' consisted in the greeting of the angel Gabriel and the greeting of Elizabeth with a later addition of the Holy Name of Jesus to conclude it. Parallel with this there was a provision of lay Psalm books – texts of Psalms with an added reference to the lives of Jesus and his mother. Out of these evolved the 'mysteries' of various numbers, 5, 10, 15 or 20, making a more and more complete series of Gospel meditations. The word 'rosarium' or rose garden was applied to the series. Tradition has handed down a fifteenth-century story of St Dominic having received the Rosary much in its present form from Our Lady herself, but research has fairly well established that the Carthusians of the fifteenth century influenced its development (see s.v. Rosary, *New Catholic Encyclopaedia*).

Originally the prayers on the beads were each prefaced with a scriptural text and later by a short meditation before the ten prayers, and later still the 'Our Father' prefaced each mystery and lastly the concluding 'Glory be to the Father' was added.

A set of beads is useful, though the gift of ten fingers means we have a built-in rosary! With our fingers outstretched and conjoined we can begin with the Lord's Prayer and then by lowering our fingers one by one we can count the ten prayers we are saying until we have interlaced fingers and then say the 'Glory be'. For those using the beads the detached bead is the initial 'Our Father' and on the series following count the ten prayers – with the 'Glory be' on the chain.

In the light of the wonderful ecumenical use of this form of prayer which, like a miracle, is happening without human fostering, it may be useful to say something about the repetition of prayer. Some think that repetition in prayer is contrary to our Lord's command not to use 'vain repetitions'. The word in Greek is 'battalogia', that is babbling – just using prayer as words which by their very number and insistence will bring the required answer. If the AV translation is used the accent is on *vain* not on repetition. Christ himself used the same prayer, 'Thy will be done', over and over again – and St Francis spent the night repeating 'My God and my All'. Prayer of this sort can be compared to the hammer taps we give to a nail so that each time we repeat the simple prayer we are driving the point home – to ourselves, into our hearts. Or it may be compared to wind again and again striking the sail of our boat as we go further into the ocean's depth.

For some, the simple name, Jesus or Mary, said in gratitude, repentance, praise or petition suits their need; for some, the mystery gives rise to the final prayer of Jesus and his church, 'Abba' – 'Father'. For most, the traditional Hail Mary on each bead allows the mind free to penetrate and reflect on the mystery, the words of the prayer forming a safety net for wandering thoughts. Slow, ruminative, restful presence in the context of the mystery will be helped by a return to the early practice of reflecting on a text before each prayer on the beads or fingers.

For Christians of other traditions, perhaps unused to this method of prayer, it may be useful to say that Catholic experience is that the mother now, as in the Gospels, always passes us on to her Son and very often with the words, 'Whatever he says, do it'.

It seems that the Holy Spirit is calling us all into the depths of simple prayer. After half a century of much change and upheaval in personal, social and political life, after so many moving icons of life on television, after so many hectic and 'driven from behind' existences, we are called in our failure, inadequacy and confusion to 'rest in the Lord'. For some, it will mean a quiet return to well-known vocal prayers; for some, a return to slow digestion of the Gospel words; for others, a direct plunge into the prayer of the Presence – almost wordless. For most of us, it will be all of these. Whatever the Holy Spirit is leading each one of us to undertake, the Rosary contains all these ways. Hurry and bustle here would defeat its object. There must be no 'account-book' attitude which the very beads and sets of mysteries could encourage in the minds of the scrupulous. One quietly unhurried contemplation of a mystery is worth all fifteen feverishly accomplished. The very purpose of the Rosary is to lead us into the Presence of our Creator, Redeemer and Sanctifier, to encourage us to rest on the shoulder of Jesus as the beloved disciple did – to rest in the Lord and receive his promise as he invites us, 'Come to me, all you who labour and are overburdened, and I will give you rest. Shoulder my yoke and learn from me, for I am gentle and humble in heart, and you will find rest for your souls' (Matthew 11.28).